Original title:
Embrace of the Northern Chill

Copyright © 2024 Creative Arts Management OÜ
All rights reserved.

Author: Ryan Sterling
ISBN HARDBACK: 978-9916-94-496-7
ISBN PAPERBACK: 978-9916-94-497-4

Through the Veil of Chilly Glare

Frosty fog wraps the trees,
Squirrels dart with frozen knees.
Snowflakes dance in a snowy swirl,
Even penguins give a twirl.

Warmth is lost, so we wear layers,
Hot cocoa is our brave prayers.
Chilly winds sing silly tunes,
While hot hands hug for warmth in the rooms.

Fractured Light in Winter's Grip

Sunlight fights through icy panes,
Icicles are nature's chains.
Snowmen stand with carrot nose,
Looking sharp in frosty clothes.

Tea is steaming, laughter flows,
Socks are tangled in winter's throes.
Dance we do, with clumsy feet,
Slipping on the icy street.

The Pulse of the Warming Chill

Breezes tease with sneaky cold,
Tales of warmth are bravely told.
Footprints crunch on the sparkly white,
While groans come from snowball fights.

Laughter echoes through the frost,
In the chill, we're never lost.
Fuzzy hats on heads do sway,
As we trip and dance our way.

Aurora's Kiss on Silent Eve

The sky bursts with a frosty glow,
Winter's beauty steals the show.
With every breath, a puff appears,
Laughter mingles with frozen cheers.

Moonlight dances on snowy drapes,
While reindeer ice-skate in funny shapes.
Hot pies bubble, fresh from the bake,
In this chill, we jump awake!

Lullaby of the Wintry Woods

In a hat too big, I strut with glee,
Frosty friends laugh, they're just like me.
Snowflakes tumble, oh what a sight,
Rolling in snow, we giggle with delight.

Trees all dressed in puffy white coats,
Squirrels in sweaters, gathering oats.
Hot cocoa steaming in mittened hands,
Winter mischief in frosted lands.

The Breath of Cold Morning Light

Morning whispers, icy and bright,
My nose is pink, what a silly sight!
Penguins slide down icy slopes,
While we sip tea and share our hopes.

Frosty windows, let's make a scene,
Draw a smile where the chill's unseen.
Laughter echoes, the sun peeks through,
Winter's a stage; let's put on a show too!

Dreams Beneath a Layer of Snow

Under a blanket, soft and white,
Dreaming of snowball fights at night.
Snowmen wobble, with carrot noses,
Next year's contest: the biggest roses!

The world is quiet, all wrapped up tight,
Snowflakes dance like confetti in flight.
Shovel in hand, I try to prepare,
But my cheeks are red, frosty and bare.

Songs of the Frigid Evening

Stars twinkle like frosty little chimes,
We gather round, sharing silly rhymes.
A hot drink in hand, we toast the night,
Winter giggles, giving us a fright.

The moon is blushing, what a fine show,
Jack Frost plays tricks that put on a glow.
While we dance on ice, slipping just so,
We laugh and we tumble, what a grand throw!

Solitude Wrapped in White

Snowflakes dance like they're drunk,
Fumbling and falling with a thunk.
Every flake's a tiny snowman,
Wishing for warmth, but who's the fan?

Sipping cocoa, lost in thought,
A frozen world, laughter caught.
Squirrels in scarves, they prance about,
Chasing their tails, with laughs we shout.

Chilling Caress of the Twilight

The twilight's touch is rather bold,
Whispering secrets 'neath the cold.
Hot chocolate spills as laughter flows,
Winter's jokes, nobody knows!

Icicles dangle like wild teeth,
Frost bitten smiles, no warmth beneath.
Snowmen strike poses, look so grand,
Filled with dreams, but no warm hand.

Echoes of the Arctic Breeze

A flurry of giggles, chilly delight,
Sneaky snowballs take flight at night.
Frosty fingers are just for fun,
Chasing the sun, oh what a run!

Breezes tickle with frosty glee,
Who knew cold could feel so free?
Under the moon with laughter shared,
Whirling and twirling, nobody cared.

Heartbeat of a Frostbitten Dawn

Morning arrives with a frosty grin,
The world wears white, let the games begin!
Icicles hang like fashion faux pas,
Who knew winter's style had such flaws?

Warm boots crunch on sparkly ground,
Echoing laughter, the best sound.
Wrapped up snug, I'll take my chance,
Frozen feet, but a twinkling dance.

Secrets of the Winter Woodlands

In the woods where snowflakes prance,
Squirrels slink in their furry pants,
Rabbits hop with a clumsy flair,
Whispering secrets to frosty air.

Trees wear white like a fashion show,
Every branch dressed in chilly glow,
Nature chuckles, a frozen jest,
As critters prepare for their winter fest.

Mice tiptoe on the icy crust,
Finding snacks in their winter trust,
With each crunch, a giggle ignites,
Sled dogs giggle at their silly fights.

In the hush of the wintry scene,
The snowmen wink with a frosty sheen,
While the owls hoot in their snowsuit pride,
The woodland's humor can't be denied.

Serenity in the Stillness of Snow

Flakes tumble down like tiny clowns,
Painting the world in sparkling gowns,
Kids slide down hills, shrieks fill the air,
As snowballs fly without a care.

Candles flicker in the frosty night,
Chill whispers offer a humorous fright,
Snowmen pretend to dance and sway,
While you wonder if they'll melt away.

A snow globe world of pastel hues,
Where winter's chill plays peek-a-boo,
Hot cocoa laughs at the frosty blow,
As marshmallows float in to steal the show.

In the quiet, the calm holds a prank,
Nature giggles in her snowy bank,
Every breath becomes misty fun,
And frozen moments shine like the sun.

Glimmers in the Frostbitten Light

Sunbeams spark on a chilly morn,
Frosty jewels on branches adorn,
Penguins slide on the frozen sheet,
In their tuxedos, they can't be beat.

The snowmen grin with carrot noses,
Dressed as if in garden poses,
While flakes tumble, they sway and shake,
In winter's waltz, they giggle and quake.

Icicles dangle, sharp as a spear,
But who needs swords? The joy is here,
With sleds that zoom and laughter bursts,
These sweet moments quench winter's thirst.

The tree branches dance in the breeze,
Nature chuckles, delightfully pleased,
In a world where the snowflakes tease,
Winter wraps us in giggles with ease.

The Enchantment of Chilled Air

Breezy whispers tickle your nose,
While winter struts in its cozy clothes,
With hats and gloves, we prance about,
In bundled laughter, there's no doubt.

Sleds glide by with a joyful cheer,
While snow angels float without fear,
Snowy mishaps turn into a show,
As laughter dances in the white glow.

Hot soup steaming, a rich delight,
Keeps you warm on a frosty night,
As squirrels play tag in the snow,
Nature's joke is on us, you know.

In this chill, there's a sense of glee,
Every snowflake sings its decree,
With whimsical moments in the fresh air,
Winter's antics are beyond compare.

A Tapestry of Winter's Hues

Snowflakes dance like little clowns,
They paint the world in silly crowns.
The trees wear coats of frosty white,
While squirrels sled down with all their might.

Laughter floats on chilly air,
As penguins skate without a care.
The winter sun, a shy old soul,
Waves farewell from its frosty shoal.

Glistening Trails in the Snow

Footprints zigzag, oh what a sight!
Looks like penguins had a food fight.
A snowman grins, his carrot nose,
Stuck in a jam with winter's woes.

A sled dog dreams of chasing stars,
While icicles hang from windows like bars.
Hot cocoa spills, oh what a scene,
Winter's mischief is quite the routine.

Sundown Over the Frozen Lake

The sun dips low, oh what a game,
Ice fishermen all shout out names.
They catch more laughs than fish today,
As seals join in the frosty play.

Skaters twirl with a comical flair,
Wobbling like ducks searching for air.
A polar bear, in shades no less,
Acts like he's on a TV quest.

The Hush of Winter's Hold

Silence blankets the world so tight,
Except for giggles under starlight.
Snowballs fly in a fluffy war,
As children choose teams and roar.

The moon peeks in, a curious guest,
To watch the chaos, it's the best.
Hot soup spills, warm jackets torn,
In this chilly jest where joy is born.

The Symphony of Stormy Skies

The clouds belt out their winter tune,
As snowflakes dance beneath the moon.
With every gust, the trees all sway,
And squirrels debate the weather's play.

A hat flies by, a mitten too,
The wind's a prankster, who knew?
It blows my scarf into a tree,
Yet all I want is hot chocolate, you see.

Icicles dangle like teeth of ice,
A slip and slide would be quite nice.
With frozen toes and red-nosed cheer,
I laugh out loud, can winter disappear?

So let it snow, let it be cold,
I'll bundle up, be brave and bold.
For every chill brings laughter's flair,
In this winter scene, I find my share.

Solitude Wrapped in White

The world outside is white and still,
Wrapped up tight like a winter's thrill.
I sip my tea, a cozy mug,
While snowflakes tease and nature bugs.

The silence sings of frosty fun,
While icicles play, oh, what a run!
The trees look like they've lost their hair,
While snowmen grin with frosty flair.

My cat leaps out with snowball glee,
Chasing flakes like they're made of tea.
With paws all cold and fur that's damp,
She plots her next ambush, oh what a champ!

So here's to solitude and white,
With giggles echoing through the night.
Laughing at winter's artsy guise,
I find my joy 'neath cloudy skies.

Cradled by Winter's Song

With chilly breath and icy feet,
The world turns round in a frosty beat.
I slip and slide on snowy ground,
And giggles echo all around.

A snowman stands, so tall, so proud,
With a carrot nose, he greets the crowd.
But wait, what's this? A snowball fight!
With laughter ringing through the night.

The hot cocoa's steaming in my cup,
As I wrap cozy clothes, all snugged up.
The winter wraps us in its fold,
With stories of warmth, happily told.

So here's to the chill, the fun, the laugh,
In every flake, a winter path.
We dance and spin in this frosty throng,
Cradled tightly in winter's song.

Whispers of Frosted Breezes

The snowflakes twirl like tiny sprites,
Dancing on air, oh what a sight!
They tickle my nose, I let out a sneeze,
Caught in their antics, I laugh with ease.

A snowman stands, looking quite proud,
With a carrot nose and a fluffy shroud.
But when the sun peeks, oh what a shame,
He melts like ice cream, forgetting his name!

The rabbits hop with a frosty flair,
Leaving prints in the white, everywhere.
They whisper secrets, so sly and fast,
But I just trip over, hoping it won't last.

So let's drink cocoa, all warm and bright,
While outside, the world turns all white.
We'll giggle and jest, in this chilly show,
For laughter warms hearts, don't you know?

Dance of the Winter Shadows

Under moonlight, shadows play,
They prance about in a silly way.
A snowdrift sways like a jolly friend,
Promising laughs that never end.

The icicles dangle, a chandelier's tease,
I walk underneath, feeling the freeze.
They jingle and jive, oh quite the sound,
As I fumble and tumble, lost on the ground!

The squirrels in mittens, all hoarding their nuts,
Mocking my clumsiness, oh what a bunch!
They chatter and squeak, having a ball,
While I'm stuck here, unable to crawl.

So come join the fun in this frosty dance,
Let's laugh at the winter, take a chance!
With every slip, we'll smirk and sigh,
For in this chill, our spirits fly!

Silence Beneath the Icy Veil

A blanket of white, it hushes the sound,
Yet giggles escape when I fall to the ground.
The trees, like statues, wear coats of frost,
In this frozen realm, I find what I've lost.

The snowflakes tease my bundled-up face,
As I chase a dog, who's won the race.
He rolls in the snow, with graceful delight,
While I just flounder, not quite upright.

Whispers of chill, they flirt with my ear,
While birds fly by, casting glances of cheer.
I wave to the sky, in this soft, silent show,
While ice-pops my tongue, so cruel and slow.

Yet in the cold, I find warmth in a grin,
Laughter erupts, letting the fun begin.
So let's sled down the hill, oh what a thrill,
In silence, we burst, with joy, just until!

Frosted Embrace of the Pines

Pines stand tall with a wintery coat,
Their branches sag, in frosty note.
I march along, feet crunching the snow,
While trying to dance, oh it's quite the show!

The squirrels, they chatter from up in the trees,
Daring me to climb, if I please.
But all I can manage is a wobbly spin,
As I tumble and giggle, oh where do I begin?

The breeze gives a jaunt, swirling the flakes,
As I flail with laughter, oh for goodness' sakes!
Each gust grips my hat, a mischievous tease,
Like winter's strong grip, making me wheeze.

So gather your friends, let's make this a blast,
With snowball fights and memories to last.
In the frosted forest, let's giggle and cheer,
Beneath the tall pines, winter's fun is here!

The Allure of Icy Boughs

Trees wear their frost coats tight,
Sparkling like disco balls in the night.
Squirrels slide down with a cheeky grin,
Wondering where their acorns have been.

A penguin waddle with a snowman's stare,
Whispers to birds that land everywhere.
"Is it cold?" they ask with puffed out chests,
Just another day for these frosty guests.

Snowflakes dance like they've had too much cheer,
While snowmen shiver, chattering near.
A snowball fight breaks out with glee,
Who knew winter brought such jubilee!

In this chilly realm, laughter takes flight,
As winter's humor shines oh so bright.
Grab your hot cocoa, don a warm sock,
Life's a snow globe, just give it a rock!

Mosaics in Winter's Breath

The sky dons a hat made of misty gray,
While kids drift off in their sleds to play.
A hot chocolate stand sells joy in a mug,
Out here in the cold, winter's a hug.

Frosty whispers of tales spun from ice,
Where cats in woolen coats look quite nice.
The laughter of children echoes and swirls,
As snowflakes tumble, like giggling girls.

Snowball chats bounce with a giggly thud,
While penguins practice their waddle and mud.
"Who slipped today?" asks the icy breeze,
As laughter erupts with delightful ease.

Each breath is a cloud that drifts and plays,
In the art of chill, we spend our days.
So take off your mittens, let's dance on the street,
In this frozen canvas, oh, life is sweet!

Chilled Hearts in a Frozen Land

In this land where frost creeps low,
Hearts thaw out with a rosy glow.
A walrus in shades dances with flair,
While igloos dress up with snowman hair.

Pinecones pop corn in the winter sun,
While snowflakes argue whose turn is to run.
Two polar bears play tug-of-war,
With a scarf that seems to stretch to the floor.

Let's wrap up in blankets, hot tea in hand,
Debating the fashion of this frozen land.
"Is it slippers or snowshoes?" we jovially quiz,
As we make snow angels with giggles and whiz.

A chorus of shivers can be heard from afar,
As even the snowmen all wish on a star.
Here's to cold days that spark with delight,
In this whimsical world, the heart feels just right!

A Horizon Wrapped in Ice

The horizon glitters with a frosty cheer,
As ice skaters twirl, their laughter we hear.
Twirling around in a pirouette spree,
While seals applaud, perched snugly at sea.

The horizon shifts and shivers awake,
With buoyant snowflakes, like sweet little cakes.
Polar bears practice their tiptoe ballet,
While penguins conga through snow in a fray.

Frosty fingers pull hats over ears,
As laughter erupts to drown out the fears.
Here in this wonder, the world is a game,
With chilly delights that never feel the same.

So raise a big mug, toast snowy sunsets,
With every cold breath, let's place our bets.
On snowball battles and furry embraces,
In this icebound land, we find joyful faces!

Chasing the Whispers of Winter

Snowflakes dance with frosty glee,
Children laughing, wild and free.
They build a fort, a throne of ice,
Claiming winter's chill as their paradise.

A snowman grins with a carrot nose,
Wearing socks that someone chose.
He tiptoes round, avoiding the sun,
In hopes of making winter fun!

The Call of Cold Winds

The wind it howls, a playful beast,
It steals my hat, it takes a feast!
A snowball flies, I duck too late,
Now I'm the target of winter's fate.

With frozen toes, I stomp and fume,
Chasing shadows that leap and zoom.
The world is white, a jolly sight,
Amidst the chaos, I laugh in spite.

In the Heart of Frosty Pines

Among the pines, the squirrels chatter,
In fleece-lined gloves, we brave the matter.
They flick their tails, I slip and slide,
While laughing critters take this ride.

A snowdrift forms, a fluffy wall,
I'm buried deep, can't hear my call!
But giggles burst from within the heap,
Winter's wonder, a sledge of sheep.

Nightfall's Icy Veil

As stars emerge, the chill arrives,
A frosty blanket, where laughter thrives.
Penguins on ice, waddle about,
Chasing their friends in a chilly rout.

A bonfire crackles, marshmallows toast,
Hot cocoa shared, we laugh the most.
With scarves unraveled, we dance around,
In this raucous night, pure joy is found.

In the Grasp of Frozen Dreams

The snow fell hard, like a clumsy friend,
Slipping and sliding, it's hard to pretend.
Frostbitten noses are all the rage,
While penguins waddle on a frozen stage.

Icicles dangle, a toothy grin,
They look like daggers but we still jump in.
Snowmen gossip in hats far too tall,
As snowflakes dance, they begin to sprawl.

Hot cocoa spills like giggles in the night,
We sip it fast, trying not to fight.
The winter wind brings a sneeze and a cough,
But laughter erupts with a warm scarf-off.

So let's embrace this chilly routine,
With ice-cube battles and jackets obscene.
We'll twirl like snowflakes under the moon,
In this frosty realm, we'll all be buffoons.

Glimmers of Light on Icy Waters

The lake's a mirror, yet I'm still spooked,
Glimmers of light? Or just my mind cooked?
I tried fishing with a frozen glove,
The fish just laughed, oh, winter's tough love.

Ice shanties pop up like mushrooms in rain,
Inside, folks are playing charades in the pain.
One fell through the hole while telling a tale,
The catch of the day? A very wet wail.

With skates on my feet, I tried to impress,
But instead, I fell and caused quite the mess.
The animals watched, both amused and bemused,
Guess winter fashion has folks simply confused.

But laughter bursts out in this lovely cold,
As stories of ice mishaps vividly unfold.
Let's twirl and slide, with joy in our hearts,
In waters of winter, where laughter imparts.

The Softest Touch of Winter's Hand

A blanket of snow hugs the ground so tight,
It tickles my toes, oh what a delight!
Pine trees decorated in a frosty embrace,
With squirrels giggling, all over the place.

I built a fine snowman, he gave me a wink,
But I whispered a secret and he started to sink.
My snowball fight was a comedic affair,
As I missed the target and got my friend's hair.

Instead of icicles, let's swap them for spritz,
With bubbles and laughter, no time for small bits.
Hot chocolate spills turn into a snowy splash,
And everyone's heart feels a bubbly flash.

So count your snowflakes and join the fun,
In winter's cocoon, we've only begun.
With shivers and giggles beneath the pale moon,
In this snowy kingdom, let's swoon and then croon.

Echoes in the Glacial Silence

In the depths of silence, I hear quite a sound,
A thud, a crunch, someone's falling down.
My mittens too bulky for this little task,
I tried to catch snow, but it's feeling quite brash.

Where's the snowman who was quite so grand?
He melted away while I tried to stand.
The howling wind, a comedic tune,
It whispers, "Chill out, just shout at the moon."

Snow angels are flopping like fish out of air,
"You've got to be kidding!" that's my winter flair.
I twirl like a snowflake, then land on my cheeks,
Laughter erupts; winter's humor peaks.

So let's gather 'round in the frosty delight,
With stories of laughs under the pale moonlight.
For in this glacial silence, we find quite the cheer,
A snowy ballet, with friends far and near.

Breath of the Frigid Horizon

Cold winds dance around my nose,
A frosty breeze, it certainly knows.
Snowflakes tumble, like clowns in flight,
Giggles echo through the frosty night.

Hot cocoa's steaming, my hands clasp tight,
Marshmallows float in a snowy white.
Sledding down hills, a winter's fun,
Now I'm just hoping to not be outdone.

Wearing mittens, each one a thrill,
But losing one? Now that's the spill.
Icicles hang like a frozen prize,
Watch your head! They're crafty little spies.

So here's to winter, with laughter and cheer,
With a snotty nose, I hold my mug near.
For every slip and frosty fall,
Creates a tale we'll laugh about all.

A Serenade to the Snowflakes

Snowflakes fall like tiny stars,
Each with its giggle, from Venus or Mars.
They tickle my nose as they play on my cheek,
What a wacky game, winter's truly unique!

With a snowman grin, I stack up the rounds,
His carrot nose flows with silly sounds.
Snowballs thrown in a comical fight,
Frosty giggles fill the chilly night.

Winter jackets make our arms look wide,
As we waddle like penguins, full of pride.
Boots are slippery, beware of the falls,
We'll laugh 'til we drop, despite the cold brawls.

But when the sun shines, to thaw out our laughs,
We'll chase each other, like playful giraffes.
For every cold moment, there's joy on repeat,
In the frosty embrace, life's laughter's complete.

Rituals of the Northern Lights

The sky bursts in colors, a wacky display,
Dancing and swirling, a crazy ballet.
Under this canvas, we laugh and we spin,
Chasing the glow, where the chill has been.

Hot tea in hand, we toast with a cheer,
To the mystic lights, we hold so dear.
A snowman contest, my nose made of cheese,
Fashion a carrot? Oh please, if you please!

Backyard bonfires bring warmth amidst frost,
Roasting marshmallows—oh, nothing's lost.
We're wrapped in our blankets, like burritos we sit,
Chortling at snowmen that look like they quit.

Each flicker of light, like a playful tease,
Makes winter's canvas spark joy with ease.
For in every giggle, and every bright swirl,
Lies the magic of winter, a whimsical world.

Veils of Ice Over Sturdy Earth

The ground adorned with glistening sheets,
Slipping and sliding, our frosty feats.
I try to walk straight but end up on my back,
Winter's slapstick is quite the knack!

With every step, a surprise awaits,
My laughter escapes, as I open the gates.
Snowflakes land like confetti on hats,
There's humor, of course, in the whole snowy spats.

Snow-covered roofs with icicles long,
A crooked design brings out the song.
For in every slip, a cool story grows,
In this chilly season, joy magically flows.

So let's raise our mugs, to the shivers and shakes,
To the chuckles and snickers that winter makes.
For every cold breath, a giggle persists,
Wrapped up in snow, we can't help but coexist.

Beneath the Silvered Pines

Beneath the pines, the snowflakes play,
They tickle the nose in a frosty way.
Build a snowman with a carrot nose,
Who'd have thought he'd wear my clothes?

Sledding down hills, oh what a sight,
I scream like a bird, frozen in flight.
But the sled gives a turn, I roll with glee,
Landing near a squirrel who looks just like me.

Hot cocoa waits, steaming and warm,
As I plot my next snowman charm.
Teacups and mittens, a fashion parade,
Who knew winter could bring such a blend?

So here's to the frost, the ice, and the fun,
Counting each snowflake like all are my sons.
With laughter and warmth, we cherish the thrill,
In a world of white that gives us a chill.

A Dance with Arctic Shadows

Snowflakes swirl in a wild ballet,
As I trip on my skates in an icy display.
The penguins beside me start to jeer,
I wish I could fly, or better yet, steer!

Branches crackle with snowy delight,
While I stagger around in the cold, what a sight!
A snowball fight starts with a mischievous grin,
And soon I'm half buried in laughter and sin.

The flurries become my icy companions,
As I dance with the chill in a flurry of canons.
But wait, I trip on a fresh patch of snow,
And land face-first, oh where did it go?

Yet still I rise, with a toothy grin,
As the arctic whispers and teases within.
With shadows that jiggle, and frost that we chase,
We spin through the evening, a laugh-filled embrace.

Frost-Kissed Dreams

In the morning light, the frost greets me,
With a wink and a nod, as wild as can be.
My boots crunch down on the crystals below,
I think I can dance, and try to put on a show.

Armed with hot chocolate, I march to the lake,
Where the ice is as thin as a hopscotch mistake.
I twirl and I glide, but oh! What a fall,
The frosty ground says, "I've got you, my pal."

Icicles dangle like diamonds on trees,
Looking lovely but sharp as a bear's angry sneeze!
I duck and I dodge while the snowflakes do tease,
Whispering jokes on the winter breeze.

But the joy never fades in this wintery land,
With mittens and scarves, we're all in good hands.
So here's to the laughter, the chill and the cheer,
In frost-kissed dreams where we shed every fear.

Echoes of the Winter Moon

The moon hangs low with a silver grin,
Reflects on the snow where our mischief begins.
In the quiet of night, we play hide and seek,
With shadows of snowmen on the ground, oh so bleak.

In socks that are mismatched, we race through the chill,
Tripping on snowdrifts over the hill.
Our laughter erupts like a snowstorm of cheer,
As the sparkling flakes fall and our worries disappear.

Inside, the hot pies bubble and burst,
While I stand by the window, feeling quite cursed.
With snowballs in hand and a grin oh so wide,
Who knew winter's tales could be a joyride?

So here's to the echoes of laughter that loom,
In the cold of the night, where the shadows consume.
We twirl 'neath the moon with hearts open wide,
In a world of soft snow, where fun cannot hide.

Reveries in a Frosted World

Snowflakes fall with graceful flair,
It's like nature's fancy fair.
Polar bears in knitted socks,
Slipping 'round on icy rocks.

Hot cocoa spills on frozen toes,
As winter's breeze does quite a pose.
Sledding down the hill so fast,
Who knew ice could bring such laughs?

Frosty breath like dragon's puff,
Running wild, it's just enough.
Snowmen sport their carrot noses,
While squirrels claim the winter roses.

A snowball fight with overkill,
A frosty duel, it's such a thrill.
In this chilly frosted land,
We laugh together, hand in hand.

Frosted Petals in a Wintry Garden

Winter blooms with frosty grace,
Petals sparkling in their place.
Time to dress in woolly gear,
And plant some seeds of chilly cheer.

Icicles hang like crystal spears,
As we giggle through our fears.
Snow bunnies hop, with clumsy style,
Jumping high, they make us smile.

Gardens dressed in white so bright,
Sneaky snowmen sneak at night.
With hats askew and scarves unfurled,
They dance around our frosted world.

Chatter of birds in winter's grasp,
Chasing warm rays, a funny task.
In this garden, oh so still,
We find warmth in our frosty thrill.

Shadows of the Northern Sky

Underneath the twilight glow,
Shadows stretch, it's quite the show.
Polar bears with witty glee,
Slide on ice like they're carefree.

Stars are peek-a-boo tonight,
Winking softly, what a sight!
Wind whispers jokes upon the frost,
In this chill, we count the cost.

Snowflakes play a game of tag,
Landing softly with a brag.
Every stomp brings laughter loud,
A frosty mischief, oh so proud.

Who knew cold could spark such fun?
With giggles shared, we are not done.
In this wonderland we tread,
Funny tales are best widespread.

The Quietude of Frozen Lakes

Lakes are frozen, glassy sprawl,
Who thought they'd play ball after all?
Ice skaters slip with flavors bright,
Twisting, turning, what a sight!

In the stillness, laughter sings,
As winter sprinkles funny things.
Thermal mugs and marshmallow hats,
Bring giggles with cheerful chats.

The crisp air bites, but we don't mind,
Funny frosty friends all aligned.
Games of charades on icy sheets,
As we skate to frosty beats.

So, let's raise a mug to the cold,
For memories made and tales retold.
In the quiet, a warmth appears,
Laughter dances, melting fears.

Encounters with the Frosted Dawn

When dawn sneezes frost on my nose,
I jump and shout at the chill that imposes.
The trees wear coats made of sparkling white,
And squirrels play tag, oh what a sight!

My coffee's frozen before it takes a sip,
I smile at the hiccups that make me trip.
The air's so cold, it tickles my cheek,
Who knew winter could play hide-and-seek?

Snowflakes dance like they've lost their way,
While I dance awkwardly, trying to sway.
The sun peeks out, but won't say hello,
It's hiding behind clouds, putting on a show!

So here I stand in a frosty daze,
Counting my toes in a wintery haze.
If laughter's the warmth that keeps us alive,
Then I'll crack up until I thrive!

Beneath the Blanket of Snow

Under a blanket thick and bright,
I lost my shoe, oh what a fright!
The snow's a prankster, soft and sly,
With every step, it whispers, 'Try!'

My nose looks red, like Rudolph's gleam,
As I plow through drifts, it's quite the dream.
A snowman grins, but it's a bit tall,
I challenged it to a snowball brawl!

The cat gives me looks, so astute,
While plotting a heist on my winter boot.
She leaps with grace, then sinks like a stone,
In this fluffy world, we're not alone!

So let's stamp around on this snowy sheet,
Where laughter and snowflakes both blend sweet.
In this winter wonderland I'll prevail,
With each frosty chuckle, I'll tell the tale!

Crystalline Lullabies

Icicles dangle, tuning a song,
As winter whispers, 'Come sing along!'
The wind plays tricks like a cheeky friend,
Who knew icy breath could make you bend?

Frosty patterns on all the windows,
Create a gallery, while the laughter flows.
The cat skids past, in a dramatic slide,
As I chuckle at winter's messy ride!

Snowflakes pirouette, a ballerina's grace,
While penguins waddle, embracing the chase.
It's a chilly ballet, with a comedic flair,
Where everyone trips, but we simply don't care!

So let's hum those tunes and have a good laugh,
In this crystalline world, we'll find our path.
With smiles and shivers, we'll make our way,
In lullabies of winter, we'll happily play!

Murmurs of the Icy Gale

The icy gale sings a frosty tune,
Tickling our noses with a winter's boon.
While the trees do the cha-cha, swaying so light,
I'm bundled up tight, what a hilarious sight!

A snowball fight erupts with great glee,
As laughter erupts, it's a wild jubilee.
Down the hill, we slide, what a rush!
It's a freeze-frame fiasco, we're all in a hush!

The stars wink knowingly from the night sky,
While frost gives my mustache a cheeky try.
Each breath comes out like a puff of white,
Turning giggles into clouds as we laugh in delight!

So gather round, friends, let's toast to the chill,
With hot cocoa smiles, we'll sip and sit still.
For in this frosty fun, life takes its spin,
With laughter and joy, let the winter begin!

Enigmas of Snow-Laden Trees

There once was a tree, thick with snow,
It wore a white hat, thought it was in a show.
Squirrels hid snacks in the branches so high,
While birds chirped, "Is it cold? Ain't that a lie!"

Underneath the flakes, a secret dance,
The tree swayed gently, as if in a trance.
Snowflakes tumbled, with laughter they fell,
Each landing softly, casting a spell.

In winter's embrace, they played hide and seek,
With no one to judge, the scene was unique.
A frozen ballet, in twirls and in spins,
Nature's own stage, where the fun never ends.

So here we gather, with mugs full of cheer,
Toast to the trees, our friends for the year.
With hats made of snow, they stand tall and proud,
In this frosty world, they sing, laugh, and cloud.

Frost's Quiet Resilience

Frost came one night, with a wink and a gleam,
Painting the world in a cold, chilly dream.
The flowers all giggled, all bundled up tight,
Whispering secrets, beneath the moonlight.

The garden wore ice, as if made of glass,
Every step made echoes, like footsteps on grass.
A rabbit in mittens, scurried away,
"Too cold for my ears!" was the price that he'd pay.

The pond wore a blanket, smooth like a sheet,
Where fish practiced skating, with nimble little feet.
Giddy and gleeful, they leaped without care,
Not a thought in their minds; it wasn't quite fair.

Resilience in snow, oh how they prevailed,
With chuckles and giggles, joy never curtailed.
In the frosty hours, when the world wears a grin,
Even winter's chill can make laughter begin!

A Song of Cold Horizons

Across the horizon, the sun did a dance,
Tiptoeing lightly, in its frozen expanse.
Mountains wore coats of the fluffiest snow,
"Who's got the cocoa?" they said, glimmering so.

With ski poles as wands, we'd glide down the slope,
Shouting with glee, it felt like pure hope.
Snowmen rolled mighty, with top hats so grand,
But no carrot for them, just a snack in each hand!

The wind gave a whistle, like it knew a joke,
As it lifted our hats, oh what a poke!
In this land of white, where laughter ran free,
Every cold breath was a song, a decree.

So let's raise a toast to horizons so bright,
Where winter hearts wander, full of delight.
In the chill of the air, with our friends at our side,
We'll sing of the cold, with joy and with pride.

The Winter's Frolic Upon Frozen Waves

Beneath a sky full of sparkling white,
The lake dressed in ice put on quite a sight.
Ice skates were laughing, each twirl was a cheer,
"Who needs sunny beaches? This chill is our sphere!"

The snowflakes participated in a jig,
While snowmen strutted, each big and each big!
With coral reef hats and scarves flapping wide,
They spun and they twirled, oh, what a wild ride!

The penguins all gathered, no fish in sight,
Decided to skate and create some delight.
"Watch this!" one shouted, as they slipped and fell,
With a humorous splash, it was comedy well!

By twilight's glow, our cheer grew so bright,
We marveled at winter, so silly yet right.
In frosty embrace, with smiles on our face,
We found magic and laughter in this snowy place.

Reflections in a Frosted Pond

A duck slips on ice, what a sight,
Flapping wildly, trying to take flight.
Frogs in sweaters, oh what a scene,
Shivering like they've caught a mean sheen.

The fish below giggle, 'What a blunder!'
As the cattails chuckle, 'Oh, what a wonder!'
Ice skaters twirl, but oh dear, they fall,
Landing with grace? Well, not at all!

Snowflakes drop, and someone sneezes,
A snowman loses his arms with breezes.
Neighbors gather for a hot cocoa spree,
While squirrels argue, 'That nut's just for me!'

Finally, the sun peeks, a warm high-five,
And everyone cheers, "We've survived, we thrive!"
Winter's antics are a frosty jest,
Making us laugh as we bundle up best.

Caress of Winter's Breath

The air is crisp, it tickles the nose,
I wear so many layers, even my toes.
Penguins in the park, waddling around,
Taking ballet lessons, graceful they're found.

A snowball fight, but watch where you aim,
You might just hit the neighbor, oh what a shame!
With laughter and shrieks, the battle rages on,
While Grandma in the window rolls her eyes with a yawn.

The dog in his sweater runs after a squirrel,
Chasing each leaf that begins to twirl.
His fur's all frosted, oh what a sight,
He's dreaming of summer, while lost in white!

At night we gather near the fire's warm glow,
Sipping hot chocolate, watching the snow.
With icy twinkles, the stars seem to wink,
As laughter surrounds, we forget to overthink.

Secrets of the Bitter Wind

The wind whispers secrets, trying to tell,
Of snowball mischief at school, oh what hell!
Frosty the snowman, with his carrot nose,
Cries, 'I'm melting!' as the warm sun glows!

Kids building castles, grand and majestic,
Collapsing before them, oh so domestic!
Penguins in velcro shoes start to dance,
Tripping and slipping, not a single chance.

The icicles hanging are spears in a war,
While critters below plot their food galore.
A cat in a hat thinks he rules the domain,
Till a gust takes him, then he's gone like a train!

Still, inside we chuckle, warm and snug tight,
With stories of mishaps, what a delight!
A winter's parade, all wrapped up with a bow,
Who knew that the cold could put on such a show!

A Tapestry of Ice and Twilight

Twilight descends, but the snow's still bright,
Kids are snow angels, what a fanciful sight.
Shimmering flakes fall like glitter and rhyme,
While dogs chase their tails, oh so out of time.

A sled rolls down, oh watch out for trees!
Laughter erupts with the chill in the breeze.
Hot cocoa spills as the mugs get too hot,
And Grandma's quilt laughs, 'You're tying the knot!'

The owls hoot softly, sharing their tales,
Of snowshoe adventures and frosty snails.
Yet the raccoons cuddle, a gang on parade,
Planning their heist, under shimmering jade.

As stars start to twinkle, the chill wraps us tight,
We gather 'round fires, sharing warmth and light.
With jokes and strange tales, the moments don't freeze,
In the heart of the cold, we find joy and ease.

Winter's Whisper Among the Pines

The pine trees stand tall, frozen and bare,
A squirrel in a scarf, quite a sight in the air.
Snowflakes are giggling, playing hide and seek,
While I sip hot cocoa, feeling quite unique.

Frost clings to my nose, a fun little prank,
My snowman's a winner, or maybe just blank.
Snowball fights rage on, with laughter galore,
Who knew winter's chill could be such a chore?

Breathe deep in the chill, feel it tickle your toes,
Hot chocolate's the answer whenever it snows.
The laughter of children echoes through the night,
As we dance by the fire, keeping spirits bright.

So here's to the frosty with chuckles and cheer,
With mittens and hats, let's toast to good cheer.
In the heart of the cold, let giggles take flight,
For winter's a festival—oh, what a delight!

Stillness in the Heart of the Cold.

The icicles shimmer like a toothy grin,
While penguins in coats waddle, ready to win.
Frost fingerprints linger on windows so clear,
I ponder their art while I sip on my beer.

The snowflakes are lazy, falling in a mess,
Sticking to boots with a look of distress.
My nose is a carrot, not quite on track,
And my hat has a mind of its own on this trek.

Frolicking felines slide on the ice,
With a meow and a tumble, oh isn't that nice?
The wind's like a joker, tickling my chin,
As I trip over snowbanks, laughing within.

So let's bundle up tight and venture out far,
Embracing the giggles, like a warm fuzzy car.
For while winter may chill and cause quite the fuss,
It's the frosty adventures that bring joy to us!

Whispers of Frosted Air

In the frosted air, where snowflakes parade,
I see birds in sweaters, fashionably displayed.
The snow whispers secrets, soft as a sigh,
While I slip on a patch, oh me, oh my!

From icicles dripping to snowmen that sway,
It's a carnival of giggles in winter's array.
The chill in my cheeks is a welcome friend,
As we frolic and tumble, giggling 'til the end.

Furry critters bartering for tasty warm treats,
While hot soup and laughter fill up our seats.
With scarves wrapped so tight, we dance through the night,
Swinging our mittens, what a marvelous sight!

So toast to the frost, let our troubles all cheer,
Winter's wild chaos will bring us good cheer.
With chuckles in thick coats, we bid chill adieu,
For the whispers of frost say, "We're here just for you!"

The Twilight of Winter's Breath

As daylight hangs low, the hues softly blend,
Frosty air frolics, as daylight does end.
In snow boots I stumble, quite stylish, you see,
While the trees wear their blankets, like it's meant to be.

The moon laughs at clouds as they drift through the night,

While snowflakes join in, making everything bright.
Like fluffy white pillows, they cover the ground,
In this whimsical twilight, joy knows no bound.

So let the wind tease with a playful, cold grip,
As I dance through the flakes, do a little flip.
The chill's not a foe, but a giggly friend,
Who tickles my toes 'til the very end.

So here's to the twilight, all sparkly and fun,
With warm mugs in hand, and the laughter begun.
For winter's a party, with joy to bestow,
In the hush of the chill, let your giggles flow!

The Heartbeat Beneath Frozen Ground

In the depths where penguins skate,
Beneath the frost, I dance, not wait.
My shivers laugh, my teeth do chatter,
Wonders bloom where cold hands scatter.

Snowflakes tickle, giggles burst,
As I face a wintry first.
The snowman smiles with carrot nose,
A frosted friend that 'snows' how it goes.

I sip on cocoa, watch the flakes,
As icy chills make jazzy shakes.
My frozen toes just tap away,
To rhythms only winter play.

So join the frost, don't hide away,
In this icy ball, let's laugh and sway.
We'll twirl and spin in chilly glee,
In winter's heart, we're wild and free.

In the Clutches of Arctic Beauty

A snowstorm tangled in my hair,
I'm caught in winter's frosty glare.
With boots that squeak and toes that freeze,
I twirl in circles like a sneeze.

The polar bears all stop and stare,
As I slip-slide like I just don't care.
With cheeks like tomatoes, red and round,
I make snow angels, flopping down.

Hot chocolate spills, oh what a scene,
My mittens go missing, what's between?
In this beauty, so cold yet bright,
I dance with snowflakes, pure delight.

Laughter echoes in the air,
As winter whispers, but I don't care.
I trip and tumble, then I grin,
Laughing, loving, let the chill begin.

Conversations with Wintry Whispers

Whispers float on frosty breath,
Sleds zip by like life and death.
Snowmen grumble with snowball fights,
While I respond with icy bites.

The trees gossip, their branches sway,
I join the chatter in the fray.
With snowflakes teasing down my nose,
I loan them warmth, as winter flows.

A penguin waddles, giving me sass,
I slip on ice, but I sure have class.
Frosty giggles echo around,
In this chilly realm, joy is found.

So let's converse with winter's script,
In frosty laughter, we get a lift.
With hugs of warmth in a snowy chill,
We find our joy, our hearts we fill.

The Stillness of Frosted Existence

Amidst the silence, snowflakes drift,
My frozen fingers play a gift.
Each flake a dancer, light and spry,
In this stillness, oh me, oh my!

The air is crisp, like a pickle pie,
I ponder why snow doesn't cry.
With every crunch beneath my boot,
I wonder who might steal my loot.

The wind whispers secrets, crafty and bold,
While icicles hang like tales untold.
With frosty hugs and shivery grins,
I dance with trees, let the fun begin.

A cozy nook awaits, I claim my chair,
With fuzzy socks, oh, what a pair.
In frosted existence, let me thrive,
For joy in winter helps me arrive.

The Frost-Kissed Pathway

Two rabbits on a frozen road,
One slipped and to the ice he glowed.
"Is this a dance?" the other said,
"Or just our feet—we're gonna dread!"

Snowflakes twirled like snowball fights,
As vermin skated in their tights.
They laughed and rolled, a furry game,
'Til one got stuck and yelled in shame!

Icicles hung like pointy caps,
Yet, no one warned the snowman chaps.
They wore their hats like autumn trees,
Until a gust brought down the freeze!

Joyous giggles filled the air,
As snowflakes tangled in their hair.
With chin up high, they took the plunge,
Dancing 'round till light began to lunge.

Lament of the Frozen River

The river sighed with icy breath,
A fish exclaimed, "Ah, this is death!"
But lo, a seal swam by for laughs,
"Don't worry, buddy, I'll take baths!"

One lonely duck quacked a sad tune,
While skaters cracked like the full moon.
"I'll glide atop, just watch my grace!"
But fell headfirst into the space.

The beavers built a banquet tight,
While squirrels debated winter's plight.
"Shall we dine on sticks or nuts today?"
"Let's nibble both, it's cold, hooray!"

Thus lingered laughter o'er the ice,
With goofy stunts and giggles nice.
In winter's hand, they found a place,
A wacky world in the wintry space.

Shadows Dressed in Winter's Garb

Shadows wandered in winter's wear,
A raccoon tried on a snowy hair.
"How do I look?" he winked with glee,
While birds chirped, "Fabulous, you'll see!"

The trees donned frosty coats so bright,
Plays of colors in snow late at night.
While squirrels played tag, dodging blizzards,
With snowballs making sure they were lizards.

Across the field, a moose tripped down,
"Next time, I'll wear my ice crown!"
The snowflakes giggled at his plight,
"Oh silly moose, dance with delight!"

Behind the scenes, a snowman grinned,
Sipping cocoa as the chaos thinned.
In this snowy jest, all's not amiss—
For winter's humor is pure bliss!

Secrets Beneath the Shimmering Ice

Beneath the surface, whispers scheme,
The fish gossip in a frosty dream.
"Did you hear about the skater's fall?
He slid and landed in snowballs' thrall!"

The ice is thick, but so's the jest,
With penguins having a waddle fest.
"Who wore it better?" they squawked in cheer,
"Oh look, it's Dave, he's lost his gear!"

A snow-cat strolled with beauty why,
Stealing the sleigh like a sly spy.
While neighbors chucked snow at their sprites,
Joy bounded forth with playful bites.

And so they spun on each icy edge,
Making memories along the ledge.
In winter's hold, they laughed and played,
While secrets beneath the frost just swayed.

The Mirth of Winter's Dance

Snowflakes whirl like tiny dancers,
Frosty breath makes winter prancers.
Socks in mittens, hats askew,
Who knew cold could bring such a view?

Snowmen wobble with goofy grins,
Jackets zipped up, let the fun begin!
Ice skates slide on a frozen lake,
Who knew winter's chill could be this flake?

Hot cocoa spills near snowball fights,
Laughter echoing through starry nights.
Icicles hang like frozen spears,
Who'd have thought frost could spread such cheers?

Snowball wars and laughter bright,
Chilly hands don't want to bite.
With each slip and slide, we prance,
Delighting in winter's silly dance!

Elysium of the Snow-Cloaked Foreground

A winter wonderland full of cheer,
Massive snowdrifts, oh dear, oh dear!
Penguin waddles on clumsy toes,
Even the snowmen strike silly poses.

Sleds zoom by with laughter loud,
Falling face-first in the powdery shroud.
Sipping soup from mismatched mugs,
While dreaming of snowball snug hugs.

Birds in fluffy coats sing their tune,
As chilly winds howl a goofy swoon.
Snowflakes land on noses quick,
Could winter be this much of a trick?

Jumpsuits zipped to the very chin,
Fashion sense lost in the wintry spin!
But who cares for style in this plight,
When snowmen and giggles make it alright?

The Lament of Winter's Grip

Oh, the woes of slipping feet,
A walk entangled in cold defeat.
Pants soaked through, joy turned to dread,
Stuck in snow, must I go ahead?

Frostbite creeping on toes so bare,
Who knew that this chill could be unfair?
The sassy wind with icy breath,
Keeps telling me I'm facing my death!

Whiskers frozen, nose so red,
I noddingly greet what's left unsaid.
The neighbor's dog in bright green gear,
Laughing at me, all warm and clear.

Yet a hot shower awaits my plight,
In the house with cozy light.
I'll laugh someday at this coldest trip,
For winter brings a funny grip!

Threads of Ice in a Tapestry of Blue

Winter's fabric, stitched in snow,
Woolly scarves that swish with a glow.
Each chilly puff a party roar,
As bundled folks race to the door.

Frozen hairdos, looking so grand,
Like porcupines lost in a band.
Hot soup spilling, laughter gleaming,
Who knew cold could be so redeeming?

With twinkling lights and snowball trades,
Snowflakes dance on the frozen glades.
A chilly cheer that breaks all doubt,
In winter's veil, we twist and shout!

So raise a mug and toast the frost,
For in this fun, there's nothing lost.
A tapestry painted with giggles bright,
In the chilly threads of winter's light!

Tundra's Soft Embrace

The snowflakes fell like confetti bright,
Frosty air made noses turn white.
Penguins waddle with a clumsy flair,
Even snowmen have a chill to spare.

Sledding down hills with squeals of glee,
Frostbite's just a minor fee.
Hot cocoa waits at winter's end,
But first, let's slide like the goofiest friend!

Icicles hanging like long, sharp spears,
Whispering secrets of wintery years.
Yeti sightings? A total hoax,
Just a cold bear telling bad jokes!

So come, let's dance on this icy floor,
With laughter and slips, we'll all implore.
For winter's chill might be a tease,
But joy is found in frosty breeze!

Fire and Ice Beneath the Northern Sky

Underneath the stars so grand,
With marshmallows in high demand.
Flames crackle bright, but chills are real,
So let's roast some treats with slippery zeal!

The moose wear blankets, looking so fine,
While rabbits hop, like they're on a line.
Snowball fights with laughter loud,
Who knew winter made us so proud?

Hot chili steams in the frosty air,
Winter's a prankster, and we must beware.
Frosty noses and giggles galore,
Who knew cold could unlock so much more?

As the night twirls in a chilly waltz,
We challenge frost with our silly vaults.
Dancing flames and snowflakes collide,
In this wild chill, let glee be our guide!

Legends of the Frigid Woods

In the woods where whispers creep,
Snowmen gather to plot and peep.
With carrot noses all awry,
They're just waiting for a snowball fly!

The trees wear blankets of icy lace,
While squirrels plan a daring race.
Frosty tales in every nook,
As winter storytellers share their book.

A bear in shades, looking so cool,
Wonders if this chill's some kind of rule.
Legends dance in flurries fast,
While winter laughs, making moments last!

So bring your mittens and sparkly glee,
In the kingdom of frost, we're all fancy-free.
With legends told by the firelight's glow,
In these frigid woods, we're never slow!

Beneath the Aurora's Dance

Under skies of shimmering jade,
Awkward penguins start their parade.
The night giggles with colors bright,
While we wear socks that don't feel quite right!

Dancing lights on this frosty playground,
Snowflakes twirling without a sound.
Sleds zooming like wild dreams crafted,
Every cozy moment, we'll leave them laughing!

With mugs of cocoa, chances we'll spill,
Underneath the northern thrill.
Laughter echoing in the crisp night,
As we slip and slide, that's our delight!

So sway with the lights, let your worries dissolve,
For in winter's charm, laughter's involved.
In this wonderland, joy is our trance,
As we wade through snow in a playful dance!

The Stillness of Crystal Nights

In the quiet of the night, it's quite a sight,
Snowflakes pirouette, in their frosty delight.
Squirrels in pajamas doing a quick jig,
While snowmen roll their eyes, just a bit too big.

The pines wear coats, oh what a scene,
Bobbing their heads to a wintery theme.
A cup of cocoa spills on the ground,
As snowballs fly all around town.

Lights twinkle softly, like stars in the air,
While penguins on skates glide without a care.
The moon gives a wink, in a frosty ballet,
As winter critters dance the night away.

So grab your mittens and join this spree,
In the stillness, buzzing like a bumblebee.
With laughter and giggles, we'll scoot and slide,
Through crystal nights, winter's silly ride.

Serenade of the Snowflake

Listen closely, do you hear that sound?
Snowflakes are singing, drifting all around.
They're hitting the rooftops like tiny drums,
While snowmen tap their feet and wiggle their thumbs.

A snowflake fairy flits and flies,
Tickling noses and painting the skies.
They twirl in spirals, a sparkling throng,
While hot chocolate bubbles, we sing along.

Hot soup is on, and laughter is too,
As frost-bitten friends cheer, "Snowball for you!"
The snowflakes giggle, as they fall with grace,
Creating a world that's a chilly embrace.

So let's raise a hat, or maybe a mug,
To flurries of joy, the season's snug bug.
And as we all dance in winter's bright glow,
We'll keep the serenade going with snow!

Hushed Echoes in the Cold

In the hush of the night, giggles start to sway,
Frost dusts the fields where snowmen play.
The moon rolls his eyes, while winter whispers,
Dancing all night with the icy twisters.

Snowshoes crunch and rabbits hop,
While frosty wind gives a cheeky bop.
Snowflakes hold court, on a frozen throne,
Ruling the winter, all on their own.

A bear in a scarf grumbles with glee,
He's traded his cave for a frosted spree.
With snowball grenades, he joins the fun,
Chasing his buddies, oh what a run!

So brace for the laughter, let the snowflakes fall,
As winter throws a party, inviting us all.
In echoes and giggles, the cold feels alive,
With cheeks all aglow, we simply thrive.

Moonlit Trails on Frozen Ground

Under a moonlight, the world looks surreal,
With trails made by sleds, an enchanting appeal.
A raccoon leads the way, with a wink and a grin,
While snowflakes giggle, as they tumble in.

Footprints create a path that is wild,
A snowman chases kids, acting like a child.
With mittens on noses and boots all askew,
We weave through the forest, a merry crew.

Thick blankets of snow, muffling each sound,
As the night wraps us in a crystal surround.
Ice skates glisten, gliding through waves,
While whispers of laughter dance in the caves.

So strap on those skates and join the ride,
Let's dance on the ice, with the moon as our guide.
In this winter wonderland, we twirl and spin,
With snowflakes our partners, let the frosty fun begin!

Milton Keynes UK
Ingram Content Group UK Ltd.
UKHW021242191124
451300UK00007B/187